GET YOUR MIND RIGHT

GET YOUR MIND RIGHT

Transform Your Life By Transforming Your Mind

TASHEANTE ROSHONDA LOCUST

CONTENTS

MESSAGE FROM THE AUTHOR

When I finally decided to stop procrastinating on the creation of this book, I realized I was withholding valuable knowledge guaranteed to change lives across the globe. It would be selfish of me, as a Certified Life Coach, to contain my insight when I know someone somewhere needs it. While my mission is to improve lives worldwide, my problem is there's only one of me. Changing lives is not easy, without stretching myself so thin, to the point there's no "me" left for me. Therefore, this book must be an extension of me, the one and only Tasheante Locust. I want this book to reach and impact women, men, and especially our youth, starting in my community. My mission with this book is to slow the progression of mental illness, relieve depression, and improve the purpose of individuals who lack confidence, self-love, and emotional stability. This book aims to build mentally strong and emotionally intelligent individuals who can use their minds to transform their lives and influence others to do the same.

By sharing their stories and experiences with this book, my readers can assist in transforming the lives of those around them by teaching them how to tap into the power of their minds when faced with adversities and uncertainties in their lives. In that regard, this book has to hit the core of my readers' souls. Every word, every phrase, every paragraph, and every page must resonate with my readers. This book has to heal my readers as they become familiar with themselves and the practices I recommend. My purpose here is not to tell you how to live your life but to teach you how to transform your mind to improve your life. For, there is always room for improvement. You may wonder, "What do you mean by 'transform my mind'?" As you read and embrace my perspective on the different aspects of life, which I believe are essential to our being. I also want you to commit to practicing the recommended tips, practices, and mental exercises. Ask and answer every question to yourself, read this book again and as often as you need to refresh your recollection. Lean on the new things you learn or realize about yourself and use them as fuel to drive change in other areas of your life and the people around you. This book is transformative. If you let it, it will transform you. As you become your higher self, be mindful of how you are and who you become along the way. Changing your mind is a long-term process. You are going to face challenges along the way. Challenges that will provoke certain emotions, which may make you revert back to your old thinking habits. Remember that you are on a journey of transformation. Remember why you picked up this book. Most importantly, remember those challenges are moments you can use to practice becoming more aware of what's happening inside of you so you can be clear and prioritize what you need to work on.

You must be diligent in your practices, determined to make a difference, and disciplined enough to complete this book and at least try every method for a minimum of 21 days. I hope you adopt new habits as you adapt to this book's methods, techniques, and mental practices. For those who like to read with a drink, I invite you to pour a glass of wine before you begin this journey. For those who don't drink wine, feel free to pour yourself a cup of your favorite beverage. Throughout writing this book, I've had a different beverage for each writing session. I've had water, tea, coffee, lemonade, and, of course, wine. So, each time you pick up this book, ensure you have a beverage that will keep you engaged with it—sip, sip.

SELF-AWARENESS

Some people may say the first step to any transformation is acceptance. I disagree. I believe the first step to an effective change is awareness, simply because you can't accept something you're unaware of. Ask yourself these questions: how aware are you of how your beliefs, habits, and natural responses affect your life? Can you name your trauma? Do you know your triggers? Do you know what triggers you? How do you show love? What kind of love do you accept? What do you like? What do you dislike? Why do you dislike those things? Do you know when you are happy? Who are you when you're with your friends, family, or alone? Think about it; what comes to mind when you think of who you are and who you want to be? Where are you? Where do you want to be? Do they align? If not, why not? What can you do right now to inspire change? Are you committed to doing what needs to be done to promote effective change in your life? Are you empowered to inspire change in others? If not, you will be by the time you complete this book and become more familiar with yourself as you adopt new thinking habits.

Pause: Go back and ask yourself each question, then answer them. To get the most out of this book, it is crucial that you actually take action on each action item listed in it. It is more than just a good read. To gain knowledge with no intent to use it is a waste of your most valuable asset, time. You have to be intentional with the knowledge you gain and be mindful of how and when you use it. You are reading this book because you know your faults, flaws, and weaknesses and are ready to elevate your life beyond this point. Or, maybe you don't know, which is an even better reason to read and finish this book. You should see what you learn about yourself as you unblock your mind throughout it. The only way to do this is to follow through with the time and effort it takes to improve your mindset about your life. Remember, it's a long-term process. You must be in it for the long run, even after you've finished this book. Sip-sip!

I hope by now you've analyzed your life and decided to actively find a way to improve it, starting with this book. See, there comes a time when you realize one of two things: either, 1) you're satisfied with your life because you are exactly where and who you want to be. You are stress-free; you have love, peace, and all the desires of your heart. You are fulfilled in every aspect of your life. Life is great, but you still feel lacking. Or, 2) you're depressed and disappointed because you are nowhere near your ideal self. You are unhappy with who you've become and where you've come to. You feel a lack of purpose like you have no reason to wake up every day. You feel like no matter how hard you try, no good ever comes of your efforts. It seems like no one sees the good in what you do, because you're only made aware of what you lack. You're regretting every decision you've ever made, and every opportunity you didn't take advantage of up to this point in your life. You feel like you're undeserving of an abundant life. You hate it here! If you can relate to this, you've likely reached a point where you feel like you're too old not to be where you want to be in life or too young to have it all figured out. That's okay because you've acknowledged where you are and realized it is not where you want to be. Picking up this book came from your motivation to finally do something about it. You're taking control of your life, and I love that for you. Sip-sip!

All you have to do now is accept these factors, decide to transform your life, set a plan, and work diligently to acquire the life you desire. Determine what's holding you back and do whatever you must to overcome it. NO EXCUSES! For, any excuse is as good as you want it to be.

Instead of focusing on the excuses that'll continue to hold you back, focus more on the ways and reasons to move forward and why you're reading this book in the first place. Are you capable of being consistently engaged with this book? What do you expect to gain from following this book's tasks and recommended practices? Are you really ready to put in the work, time, and effort it'll take to transform your life and stay consistent until you see change and beyond? I think YOU CAN. In fact, I think YOU WILL because YOU ARE! I believe in you, and you should too! Sip-sip!

Don't be an obstacle in your way. You have to be open and willing to accept harsh truths and perspectives of yourself. You must be ready to hear them outside of yourself. Meaning, you must be open and receptive to these truths from someone you'd rather not hear them from. I say that because it's easy to disregard the perspectives of others about yourself when the person delivering them is someone you hate, despise, or envy. You have to be so hungry for the life you desire that you are willing to marinate in discomfort for a while as you figure yourself out. Pay attention to the thoughts that come to mind and the feelings you feel inside as you listen to a different version of your truth come from someone else. Keep in mind, what may be true FOR YOU may not be true TO THEM, and what may be true FOR THEM may not be true TO YOU.So, don't attach yourself to any of the thoughts or feelings you witness as you listen. Acknowledge them, and let them go. Try not to attach any meaning, person, or circumstance to them. Just acknowledge and let go. Acknowledge your thoughts and let go. Acknowledge your feelings and let go.

I emphasize acknowledging and letting go to express the importance of the practice, which is essential to making a lasting impact. It's about learning, recognizing, and accepting who you are and how you show up in the world. After you've accepted these new perspectives of your truth, take time to yourself to really think about what was said, acknowledge the thoughts and feelings that arise. Acknowledge the actions you're tempted to take. Just feel and acknowledge what each thought does to your body. What are you thinking now? What are you feeling now? What beliefs about yourself was challenged the most? Have any new beliefs arisen? What do you think about yourself now? What do you think about your life experience now? What are you thinking about doing now? Just ask yourself these questions out loud, then wait for the answer to come to the forefront of your mind. Remember, the answers are already in you. You're just doing the work to become familiar with the thoughts and ideas that reside in your subconscious mind, essentially becoming more aware of why you are the way you are. This practice is best done repeatedly in silence in a dark or low-lit room (for those who are afraid of the dark). It minimizes all of your senses so you can focus inward, allowing you to recognize your thought patterns to get to the root of your behavior and start making the necessary adjustments to adopt and maintain a new mindset as you work to improve your life. It's time to take responsibility for your life. It's time to open up your mind and focus on what will elevate you.

Remember you are a combination of thought experiences, most of which only happened in your subconscious mind, therefore you've been completely unaware of the thoughts that are creating certain aspects of your life. No matter what you may have gone through in your past, the condition of your mind in those moments altered your personality and, therefore, created your personal reality. It's time to take action and regain or get control over your life. That starts with being conscious of your unconscious thoughts. If you've analyzed your life, become aware of and have now accepted where you are currently, and are ready to work to fulfill your potential, strengthen your mind, expand your purpose, and advance your life. If you're prepared for a life of abundance and you are done sitting around waiting for a miracle. If you believe you have what it takes to complete this book and transform your mind, take a sip with me as you proceed to the next page of this new chapter in your life called, Growth Journey. Sip sip!

DEPRESSION

I am a firm believer in the fact that medication is not the only cure for depression. Any person battling depression is already equipped with everything they need to overcome it. All they have to do is tap into the power of their mind. Yes, that's right. If you currently consider yourself depressed, your mind is all you need to cure it. You must first know, depression is a mood disorder. Let's break that down for a second. A mood is a temporary state of mind or feeling. Keywords: "temporary state of mind." A disorder is a disturbance in the normal functioning of the mind and body, which causes confusion. Keywords: "disturbance in the normal functioning of the mind and body." Depression impacts how you feel, think, and behave, and it's usually caused by some sort of physical and emotional trauma. Trauma is caused by a disturbance whether to your mental, emotional or physical being. Trauma has no age limit, and it surely does not discriminate against race, culture, or gender. Anyone who experiences a traumatic event in their life has to live with the emotional response as a result of it. Sometimes the emotional response lasts for years, causing them to lose their sense of safety in environments where they used to feel safe. They eventually lose their sense of self which begins to show up in their relationships as they get older, provoking more emotional instability. Trauma is a great cause of depression. Something you endured in your past caused a chemical reaction in your brain that prevented you from thinking your way out of that traumatic event. Trauma causes distinct changes to happen to the brain. Some of those changes cause parts of the brain to become resistant to change. Your survival mechanism is disturbed, your emotional responses are delayed, and your behavior displays accordingly. I tell you this because you have to be aware of the cause and effects of depression before you can consciously combat it. You must know what is affected and how it is affected to understand what you'll need to do to overcome it. It is important to know depression is a mind killer. The worst thing about it is, so many people turn to anti depression medication to cure their depression, when in fact antidepressants are also mind killers. Hear me out. Sip-sip.

Now don't get me wrong; some anti-depressants make

a difference for some people. I want you to please know and understand that antidepressants are just psychoactive substances. These psychoactive substances are mind-altering drugs that enter your brain to modify your thoughts, feelings, and behaviors. Not only do you get a temporary fix, but you are guaranteed to cause more bodily harm, better known as side effects. Firstly, I call it a temporary fix because that's what it is. It alters your thoughts, feelings, and emotions long enough to make you believe the depression has passed, usually lasting 4 to 7 days. As the antidepressant wears off, your brain will return to its prior state before the medication took present.

When your brain reverts to its original state, your thoughts, feelings, and emotions follow, eventually returning you to depression. Those who don't put in the mental work themselves to keep depression buried will quickly fall back into it. For some people, it'll be more profound. That is because they rely on antidepressants to do all the work. That's why those who take it have to take it continually. For some people, for years. Now, don't get me started on the side effects. I'm talking about sleep deprivation, nausea, weight gain, headaches, drowsiness, and feeling anxious all the time. These side effects alone are enough to drag you into an even deeper depression. That's why some people who are battling depression also have terrible anxiety. You can take my word for it or do your own research. Either way, you will realize that you already have everything within you to do the same thing an antidepressant does without the adverse side effects. If you choose to take an antidepressant regardless of these facts, just make sure you are doing the mental work to help it help you. When a negative thought creep into your mind, respond with a counter perspective, a more positive thought. You have to do this every time you get a negative thought, feeling, or feel like you need to express yourself physically. You must be intentional with your thoughts to not only combat the harmful effects of the antidepressant but also enhance its benefits. It may sound absurd and impossible initially, but it is true and can be true for you, too. Sip, sip.

Depression is something else, isn't it? It makes you sit down and think about all of your life experiences, choices, and decisions that led you to the moment you realized you were battling depression. For some, you are unaware that what you are experiencing is a bout of depression. When you are depressed, you feel weak, small, and powerless. You're constantly down on yourself, asking questions like "Why is this happening to me?", "what have I done to deserve this?" "why is this only happening to me?". Questions like these keep you stagnant and drag you deeper into depression. It's time you decide if you are the creator of your life or the victim of your life. If you believe you create your life, you must know your thoughts are what's creating it. Your beliefs about yourself and how you appear in the world create your outer reality. Being the creator of your life is knowing who and what you are and being grateful for it. The secret is in gratitude. The secret is knowing your thoughts create your reality and intentionally thinking positive thoughts even when you have reasons not to.

Focusing on nothing but the negatives or blaming yourself for things that happen outside of you are the key components that will keep you buried in depression. Thinking about everything negatively is the unhealthiest habit you can have. A negative mindset creates a negative lifestyle- full of pain, sorrow, and turmoil. Suppose good things are happening around you, and you're only focused on the negative. In that case, you are training your brain to think and create more negative thoughts, feelings, emotions, and experiences. You are training yourself to believe that there is no good around you, nothing good is happening to you, and nothing good will ever happen for you. So when you experience a positive and uplifting moment, and you find yourself thinking, "This is too good to be true," "Something is bound to go wrong," "This looks like a setup," or you start to focus on the negative "what-ifs," know that it is because of how you've conditioned your mind up to that point. This type of mindset will eventually lead you into depression. Sadly, some people are addicted to negative thinking and negative emotions. So much to the point it's become unconscious behavior. Second nature, even unknowingly creating more of it in their lives. What you focus on the most will show up in your life. If you hold a thought long enough, accompanied by a strong feeling, you will see it appear in your life. Whether you're thinking grateful thoughts or only focused on what you lack, you create your life and, therefore, will see more of whatever you're thinking about.

The most common unconscious behavior is verbalizing negative thoughts, feelings, and beliefs. When you do this, you unconsciously plant negativity in your life, eventually blossoming into more negative thoughts, feelings, emotions, and experiences. Here is a self-aware moment. Take a sip, then take a minute to reflect. How often are you speaking negatively? When did you last have a genuinely happy moment and only thought negatively? What kind of negative things do you say to yourself? What kind of negative things do you believe about yourself? How often are you complaining? Whether it's about yourself, your job, your neighbor, your significant other, or your cat, you are externalizing and creating the exact life you don't want. With that said, words are powerful beyond the average human's understanding. You have to practice thinking more positively about the happenings in your life. Even in moments that breed negative thoughts, emotions, or behaviors, you must challenge yourself to think positively and find the good in what's happening. Find a way to be more hopeful for the outcomes of your circumstances instead of continually harping on the specifics and negatives of it.

Writing down your negative thoughts, beliefs, feelings, and emotions is the best way to start. Then, write out two positive thoughts, feelings, and emotions for each one. Read this new list every day for at least 21 days. You can even do it standing in the mirror. Watch how much your life transforms just by intentionally changing your mind about how you view your life. That is how you will build the person you want to be so that you can live your desired lifestyle. You see, the power is in your intentional thinking. The emphasis is on YOU! You have the power to change your own life! If your life is not changing, it's because you are not changing. Sip, sip!

It is true that no matter how great things may seem or how happy you think you are, when you are left alone with yourself, marinating in truths you are too afraid to face, depression will creep in to pollinate your mind and suck the life out of you. But you can beat it! How? First, believe you have the power, strength, and ability to overcome depression. With belief in yourself and the power of your mind, you can pull yourself out of any traumatic experience or circumstance and begin to live a life far more significant than you ever imagined. You were born a winner. You have to know and believe that. You have to know that for most people, depression is self-inflicted. Why do I say that? Because if you are battling depression, you're unintentionally, sometimes unconsciously, generating intense thoughts and emotions that are working against you. You must become aware of this and intentionally think more positive and hopeful thoughts opposite of what you're currently experiencing. For every negative thought, follow it up with two positive thoughts. Think it twice; say it twice. You can even take a step further and write it twice. You have to do this on a continuous basis. I guarantee you will see and feel the effects of this powerful exercise within days. Yes, days! Sip, sip!

SELF-LOVE

astering self-love is the next step to transforming your life and fulfilling your purpose. You have to love yourself more than you want to be loved by others. You have to know and believe that you are worthy of more than you think you're worthy of. To love yourself, you have to give yourself everything you expect to receive from other people. If you don't receive or feel what you desire at any moment, nobody's to blame but you. Self-love is the best and only love you can give and receive simultaneously. Think about it; you already know what it feels like to love and be loved by someone else. Imagine all that love energy transpiring within you. How do you think you would feel? What's stopping you from feeling that way right now? If you don't know what it's like to experience love in any form, you will by the end of this book. Self-love may not be easy to grasp at first, primarily if you were never taught how to love, let alone how to love yourself. I've asked many people my favorite question, "How do you love yourself?" and it's caught them off guard every time. Some people would go on and on about what they do for others but never once mention what they do for themselves.

See, we have to normalize self-love. You can teach yourself to love yourself more by meditating, reading, standing in the mirror, repeating affirmations, smiling, and hugging yourself. I highly recommend the mirror action because it's so powerful. Another one of my favorite homemade methods is self-reciprocating. Self-reciprocating simply means to do for yourself the same thing you do for others. If you buy someone a gift, get yourself something of the same value or more. If you go out of your way to make someone happy, do the same for yourself. Do something for yourself that will make you the happiest you've been in a while. You are as worthy of your love as anyone else. Please know that you are MORE worthy! Sip Sip!

You have to fall so deeply in love with yourself that nothing and no one could ever interrupt how you love in general. You must be mentally able to soothe your soul and pull yourself out of the dark, mainly because you know yourself better than anybody else. You've become aware of your triggers and natural responses to certain things and people. Therefore, you have to take control and responsibility for yourself, your words, thoughts, actions, and emotions. Give no outside force the power to take you out of your element. Remember who you are and who you desire to be. Keep yourself grounded no matter how hard it is to do so. Love yourself by protecting your inner peace. You are on a journey to a life of abundance, a life of overflow of things you never thought you'd ever achieve because of your current circumstances. All I ask is, as you go through what you're going through, make sure you're growing too. Make sure you are looking out for your future self because no one will ever love or do for you as you will. You must make sure you love yourself how you desire to be loved because people treat you how you treat you. You have to celebrate your triumphs. You have to grow through your circumstances, regardless of who is watching or who cares.

We cannot improve our purpose or achieve our desired happiness by depending on someone else to permit us to follow our dreams. Accompanied or alone, we have to take action and accountability for our own lives. Some people will slander, taunt, and discourage you until you give up simply because they don't want or can't stand to see you winning. That is where internal peace and grounding come into play. They both allow you to receive the message without allowing the message to affect your decision-making, without allowing it to interrupt your inner peace. Possessing the skill to remain deeply serene amidst chaos and negativity is a powerful skill that helps your mind, body, and spirit stay consistently aligned. If you want to manifest your dreams, you must master your mind. That means learning how to use it and not allowing it to use you! I don't know about you, but I had to take a sip for that one! So many people are so internally isolated that they've become a victim of their own minds. Some people are simply unaware of this mental disconnect.

In contrast, others are aware of the mental disconnection but either refuse to acknowledge it or are afraid to. You must heal what needs to heal. Don't be scared to dig a little deeper and change what needs to be changed. Not doing this stunts your growth and limits your abilities, keeping you stuck in the position you're trying to outgrow. Refusing to heal what hurts leaves room for you to continue to hurt. You've heard the saying, "Hurt people hurt people." That's because it's true. Going through life with unresolved trauma and unhealed hurts will have you hurting people who didn't hurt you. Buried hurt will make you defensive. It will have you seeing life through a lens of pain rather than a lens of peace.

Step into your truth, be open and honest with yourself, and give yourself the gift of happiness. Take this moment to acknowledge who you had to become to grow through what you went through. Forgive yourself for carrying those survival techniques from your traumatic experiences throughout childhood and adolescence into adulthood. Hug yourself and tell yourself "I love you" because self-love is the best love. You need you! You need to know you are loved and valued by you in order to elevate your mindset so you can upgrade your life. Take a couple of slow, deep breaths and allow your body to marinate in self-love for a moment. Smile, and think about all the things that make you happy. Breathe in. When you've reached the peak of your last inhalation, inhale just a little more. Hold it for 5 seconds and let out an audible sigh so loud that you feel the vibration of your voice in your chest as you exhale. Do this 2 more times. After you've completed this breathing exercise, you will feel lighter as though a weight has been lifted off your shoulders, chest, back, and head. You'll feel more open to love and all of its forms. For most people, you may even feel freed from the barriers in your mind, which is why you may feel a little lightheaded. You've just cleared your mind and opened it up for more love and positive thoughts to take up residence, thus creating new neural pathways in the brain that will lead to more opportunities to love and be loved.

Mastering self-love is not just a journey; it's a profound transformation of your entire being, a revolution in how you perceive yourself and interact with the world around you. It's about recognizing your own worthiness, not just intellectually, but on a visceral level where every cell in your body resonates with the truth of your inherent value.

To embark on this journey of self-love, start by embracing radical acceptance of yourself. This means acknowledging your flaws, your past mistakes, and your imperfections without judgment. Understand that these aspects of yourself do not diminish your worth; they are simply part of your unique human experience. Practice forgiveness, both for yourself and for others who may have contributed to your pain or self-doubt. Release the burden of resentment and grudges, and allow yourself to step into the freedom that comes with forgiveness.

Cultivate a daily practice of self-care that nourishes your body, mind, and spirit. This could include simple acts like taking a walk in nature, indulging in a luxurious bath, or spending quiet time journaling or meditating. Prioritize activities that bring you joy and fulfillment, and make them non-negotiable parts of your routine.

Challenge the negative self-talk that may have become ingrained in your psyche over the years. Whenever you catch yourself engaging in self-criticism or self-doubt, pause and consciously reframe those thoughts with compassion and kindness. Affirmations can be powerful tools in this process, reminding yourself of your inherent worthiness and capability.

Surround yourself with people who uplift and support you on your journey toward self-love. Cultivate relationships that are built on mutual respect, authenticity, and vulnerability. Set boundaries with those who drain your energy or undermine your sense of self-worth, and prioritize your own well-being above all else.

Remember that self-love is not a destination but a continual practice. Be patient and gentle with yourself as you navigate the ups and downs of this journey. Celebrate your progress, no matter how small, and recognize that each step you take toward loving yourself more deeply is a victory worth honoring.

As you cultivate a deeper sense of self-love, you'll find that your relationships naturally begin to transform. You'll no longer seek validation or approval from others because you'll know that your worth comes from within. Instead, you'll be able to offer love and compassion freely, without expectation or attachment. Your relationships will become more authentic, more fulfilling, and more aligned with your truest self.

So take a moment to reflect on how far you've come on this journey of self-love. Acknowledge the courage and resilience it has taken to confront your fears and insecurities, and honor the progress you've made. You are worthy of love, you are deserving of happiness, and you have the power to create the life you truly desire. Sip-sip, my friend, and toast to the beautiful journey of self-discovery and transformation that lies ahead.

RELATIONSHIPS

"Why aren't relationships lasting anymore?" has been one of many posts constantly recycled on social media. Seeing the thoughts, theories, and ideas people have come up with in the comments section has been really intriguing. You have those who believe it's the women's fault, those who see men at fault, and those who think "relationships are dumb anyway." The endless stream of opinions and theories on social media only scratches the surface of a deeper issue. Amidst the blame and cynicism, there lies a fundamental truth: relationships falter when individuals within them cease to grow. Relationships shouldn't be as complex as people make it seem. They are not static entities but living, breathing entities that evolve alongside the individuals involved. Yet, all too often, we neglect our own growth, expecting relationships to flourish on autopilot. But the truth is, the foundation of any lasting relationship begins with the foundation of the self. It starts with a journey of self-discovery and self-awareness, wherein we confront our fears, insecurities, and past traumas. Only by understanding ourselves can we hope to understand and connect with others authentically, especially romantic partners. Sip-sip!

So, how do we embark on this journey of self-discovery? It begins with introspection and reflection. Take a moment each day to sit in silence, away from the distractions of the world, and delve into the depths of your mind. Ask yourself the tough questions like: What are my core values? What are my greatest fears? What patterns do I see repeating in my life? What makes me feel uncomfortable or violated? How do I want to be treated by others? What are my limits when it comes to relationships, work, or personal space? What are my non-negotiable values and beliefs?

By confronting these truths, we lay the groundwork for personal growth. Self-discovery is not a solitary endeavor. It requires vulnerability and openness with those we care to share our time with. Share your journey with trusted friends or loved ones, and encourage them to do the same. Through honest dialogue and mutual support, we can cultivate deeper connections and foster an environment that promotes growth. Yet, communication alone is not enough. We must also cultivate empathy and compassion towards others. For empathy bridges the gap between individuals, fostering deeper connections and mutual understanding. Take the time to truly listen to those around you, seeking to understand their perspectives and experiences.

When embarking on a romantic relationship, laying a strong foundation is paramount for long-term success. Certain conversations are crucial for clarifying expectations, values, and goals, ensuring alignment and mutual understanding from the outset. Initiate conversations with your partner about your individual goals, values, and visions for the future. Discuss topics such as career aspirations, family dynamics, and long-term plans to ensure compatibility and alignment. For example, if marriage and starting a family are important to you, express these desires openly and invite your partner to share their perspective.

Vulnerability is the key to fostering intimacy and trust in romantic relationships. Share your fears, insecurities, and past experiences with your partner in a safe and supportive environment. For instance, if you have a fear of abandonment stemming from childhood experiences, open up to your partner about these feelings and explore ways to support each other emotionally. By embracing vulnerability, you deepen your connection and strengthen the foundation of your relationship.

Having those essential conversations and asking yourself those core questions helps you learn more about yourself and what you're willing to tolerate in your relationships. It'll also teach you more about your romantic partner and their true intentions. It gives you both the chance to ask and answer questions like, why do you want to be with me? What do I do for you? What do you bring to the relationship? If we lost everything today, what would we have left? How have past relationships shaped how you are with me? Do you want kids? How many kids do you want? Do you want to get married? How much debt do you have? What are your career goals? How well do you handle money? What motivates you? What makes you happy? Do you believe in a higher power? Do you go to church? What are your long-term goals? What are your short-term goals? Where are you going? Do you have leadership skills? How do you handle challenges? How do you love yourself? What do you expect from me? What do you want out of this relationship? What is our purpose in being together? This question is a good one, especially for those couples who see marriage in their future. When you're with the right person, your relationship extends beyond you and your person. It becomes more significant than both of you as it takes on a life of its own. In a sense, it becomes bigger than you and you have to accept all that comes with the higher purpose of your union.

Knowing the purpose of your union will guide every

aspect of your being as you grow and elevate through life individually and together. When there is a greater purpose that expands beyond your understanding, that is when you know for sure you are on the right path, whether in love or life. You and your partner will become different individuals as you pursue the greater purpose of your placement in each other's lives. You're going to have disagreements, and you're going to run into little obstacles along the way, but you must remember who you are and what kind of experiences, background, and beliefs you come with. Mindfulness is especially important because, in a relationship, we tend to forget to look inward as we continually look outward and judge what's in front of us. It's unfair to hate or dislike your partner's flaws and faults when you know you come with your own. The one thing you need to remember when you find yourself judging your partner is you attract who you are. I don't know if you've heard the phrase "Don't be a nickel out here looking for a dime," but Lyfe Jennings dropped a bar when he said it in his song, Statistics. It's because it's true. You have to make sure you are or are becoming, the kind of person who deserves the things you desire in a relationship. You can't judge your partner's flaws and expect yours to be accepted or overlooked. That's why it's important to practice empathy.

In addition to empathy, practicing gratitude can also transform our relationships. Starting today, take a moment each day to reflect on the blessings in your life, both big and small. Express gratitude to those who have touched your life, whether through a heartfelt conversation or a simple thank you note. Gratitude cultivates positivity and strengthens the bonds of connection between individuals. But perhaps the most transformative aspect of relationships lies in their capacity for growth and change. As we journey through life alongside our loved ones, we are inevitably shaped by their presence. We must embrace the challenges and obstacles that arise, viewing them as opportunities for growth rather than roadblocks to happiness. Sip-sip!

Treat people how you want to be treated is the golden rule in life. The golden rule in a relationship is don't do anything you wouldn't be ok with if your partner was to do it. Above all, remember that relationships are a journey, not a destination. They require patience, dedication, and a willingness to evolve alongside each other. By prioritizing personal growth and fostering genuine connections, we can create relationships that withstand the test of time.

So, the next time you find yourself questioning the state of your relationships, remember that true change begins from within. Embrace the journey of self-discovery, cultivate empathy and gratitude, and above all, cherish the connections that enrich your life. For it is through these transformative practices that we can build relationships that truly stand the test of time.

Powerful relationships are the key to personal growth and fulfillment. In a world bustling with technological advances and social media connections, the essence of true human connection often gets lost in the noise. Yet, relationships, whether romantic, familial, or platonic, remain the cornerstone of our existence. They shape our experiences, influence our perspectives, and ultimately define who we are.

Healthy relationships serve as pillars of support, nurturing our emotional well-being and fostering personal growth. They provide us with a sense of belonging, acceptance, and love, essential ingredients for leading fulfilling lives. Whether it's the warmth of a familial embrace or the camaraderie of trusted friends, these connections enrich our lives in profound ways. One crucial aspect of cultivating healthy relationships is the art of active listening. Too often, we find ourselves absorbed in our own thoughts and opinions, failing to truly hear what others have to say. Practice active listening by maintaining eye contact, asking clarifying questions, and reflecting back on what the other person has shared. By demonstrating genuine interest and empathy, we can deepen our connections and strengthen our relationships.

Empathy lies at the heart of healthy relationships, allowing us to understand and resonate with the experiences of others. Cultivate empathy by putting yourself in someone else's shoes, imagining their thoughts, feelings, and motivations. For example, if a friend expresses frustration over a difficult situation at work, imagine how you would feel in their position. By acknowledging their emotions and offering support, you demonstrate empathy and strengthen your bond.

While relationships thrive on connection and intimacy, it's essential to establish healthy boundaries to safeguard our well-being. Boundaries delineate where we end and others begin, ensuring that our needs and values are respected. Whether it's communicating our limits or asserting our autonomy, setting boundaries is essential for maintaining healthy relationships. Otherwise, we'd find ourselves constantly hurting and recovering from being taken advantage of, taken for granted, or even taken out of our element. This is usually caused by a lack of boundaries, which allows things to happen that our boundaries are meant to protect us from. It's important to not only know your boundaries, but to maintain them. If you overstep your boundaries, you allow room for others to overstep them and take advantage of you.

Communicate Your Boundaries! The best way to do that is by taking the time now to identify your personal boundaries. After you've clearly identified them, you must communicate them clearly to those you want or need to set boundaries with. For example, if you value alone time to recharge, express this need to your partner or family members. You protect yourself from disrespect, heartbreak, and misunderstandings, while also filtering how far certain people can get with you. By setting boundaries, you empower yourself to prioritize self-care and maintain balance in your relationships.

Assertiveness is also a key skill in navigating relationships with confidence and clarity. Practice asserting your needs and preferences in a respectful yet firm manner. For instance, if a colleague consistently interrupts you during meetings, calmly assert yourself by saying, "I value your input, but I'd appreciate it if you could let me finish speaking before sharing your thoughts." By advocating for yourself assertively, you foster mutual respect and understanding in your relationships.

In conclusion, healthy relationships are the bedrock of our emotional well-being and personal growth. By practicing active listening, cultivating empathy, setting boundaries, and engaging in open and honest communication, we can nurture meaningful connections in every aspect of our lives. Whether it's strengthening familial bonds, fostering friendships, or cultivating romantic partnerships, prioritizing healthy relationships enriches our lives and brings us closer to fulfillment and happiness. Sip-Sip!

FORGIVENESS

ou have to learn how to forgive before you can fully and truly forgive. If you choose not to forgive a particular person or situation for whatever reason you think is valid enough, you lack the knowledge behind the power of forgiveness. Forgiveness is never about or for the other person. It's never about you taking all the blame and accountability for the entire situation. It's about YOU setting the tone for YOUR inner peace, PEACEFULLY! Think about it; what are your beliefs about forgiveness? How forgiving are you? Do you forgive easily, or do you hold grudges? Did you know forgiveness can significantly impact your life? What if I told you you could use forgiveness to improve your life? See forgiveness, giving or receiving, will always positively impact your life. The more you forgive, the easier it is to love and be loved. Forgiving is one of the most powerful tools you can use to elevate yourself out of depression, improve your self-esteem, and gain more satisfaction in your life overall. The transformative power of forgiveness composes a path to inner peace and liberation.

Forgiveness is a profound act that transcends the bounds of time and circumstance, offering us a pathway to liberation and inner peace. It's a tool that, when wielded with intention and understanding, has the power to transform even the most challenging situations. Let's delve deeper into the essence of forgiveness, exploring its impact on our lives and practical strategies to cultivate it.

It's important to understand the essence of forgiveness. Forgiveness is not about condoning the actions of others or forgetting the pain they may have caused. Instead, it's a conscious choice to release ourselves from the grip of resentment and anger. It's about recognizing that holding onto grudges only perpetuates our suffering, while forgiveness sets us free.

One of the most significant aspects of forgiveness is learning to forgive ourselves. We often carry the weight of past mistakes and regrets, allowing them to shape our present and future. However, by extending compassion and understanding to ourselves, we can break free from self-imposed limitations and embrace personal growth.

Start by acknowledging your mistakes without judgment. Reflect on what you've learned from these experiences and affirm your worthiness of self-forgiveness. Write yourself a letter of forgiveness, expressing compassion and understanding towards your past actions. Then, work on forgiving the situation.

Life is full of challenges and adversities, some of which may leave us feeling betrayed or wronged. However, holding onto resentment towards the situation only prolongs our suffering and hinders our ability to move forward. By choosing to forgive the situation, we reclaim our power and open ourselves to new possibilities.

Practice shifting your perspective by focusing on the lessons learned from the situation rather than dwelling on the pain it caused. Practice gratitude for the growth and resilience it has instilled in you. Engage in activities that bring you joy and fulfillment, reinforcing the belief that you are not defined by your past experiences.

Perhaps one of the most challenging aspects of forgiveness is extending it to those who have wronged us without remorse or apology. However, holding onto resentment only burdens us further, while forgiveness empowers us to reclaim our peace of mind. Practice empathy by putting yourself in the other person's shoes and considering the factors that may have influenced their actions. Recognize that forgiveness is a gift you give yourself, releasing the grip of bitterness and resentment. Focus on cultivating compassion and understanding towards others, recognizing that everyone is on their own journey of growth and healing.

Forgiveness is a potent tool that has the potential to transform every aspect of our lives. It liberates us from the shackles of the past, allowing us to embrace the present moment with clarity and grace. As Nelson Mandela aptly said, "Forgiveness liberates the soul; that is why it is such a powerful weapon."

By integrating forgiveness into our daily lives, we unlock the door to inner peace, personal growth, and profound transformation. It's not about erasing the past but transcending it, choosing love and compassion over resentment and anger. So, let us embark on this journey of forgiveness, knowing that with each act of forgiveness, we reclaim our power and embrace the fullness of life's potential. Sip-sip!

POSITIVITY

hy is it so hard for people to just be positive? Why is it so much easier to lean into negativity and sit back on positivity? Just think about it. Whenever you've experienced an unexpected challenge or adversity, remember how easily you conformed to the negative thoughts and feelings that arose. What did you do after becoming angry, upset, or majorly disappointed? Did your actions match your attitude? Did you act and speak out of anger? Did your thoughts and actions make the situation worse? This is usually the case when we conform to negative energy. Our behavior matches, and our problems worsen. That's why becoming aware of yourself is essential to opening up your mind so you can actively change it to improve your life. When you're in the midst of a storm, and you feel yourself getting mad, angry, or upset, if you even hear your voice rising, consciously choose to stop and think. You can either become irate, potentially worsening the situation. Or you can choose to be positive and hopeful regardless of how bad things may seem, knowing the storm will pass and the sun WILL shine again. As long as you put in the work to come out on the other side of your circumstances.

Some of you may have heard the saying, "Don't cry over spilled milk." For those who haven't, it simply means there's no sense in getting upset, mad, or angry over something that has already happened and can't be changed. You can sit, moan, and complain about every little mishap in your life, or you can encourage yourself to get over it right away so it doesn't consume your mind and cause you to conform to the negative thoughts and emotions that come with it. Yes, it really is that easy. It can all be so simple if we just actively use our minds instead of allowing it to run on autopilot. Just as easy as it is to be mean, nasty, angry, or rude, it should be just as easy to be positive, hopeful, calm, and glad that you've made it through so many moments past that one that intended to drown you in negativity.

Most of the time, something terrible or nearly traumatic happens, and our minds instantly retreat to the worst-case scenario, causing us to act accordingly. I get compliments daily about my calm and relaxed nature, especially when I exhibit them during chaotic or hostile situations. That's because I've mastered the ability to stay positive, relaxed, calm, and hopeful that the best will come out of the situation, regardless of how challenging, chaotic, or hostile it may be. Most of the time, something terrible or nearly traumatic happens, and our minds instantly retreat to the worst-case scenario, causing us to act accordingly. I repeat this because we have to become more aware of this in order to make an effective change to our mentality and attitude regarding our adversities.

When things don't work out exactly how we want them to, we tend to focus on the specifics instead of developing a new plan to get us closer to our desired outcome. Harping on the particulars of a negative situation will keep you in a negative mood and cloud your mind with negative thoughts, feelings, and behaviors, whether panicking, crying, worrying, or hysterical, making the situation harder to bear. Constantly verbalizing what happened, what went wrong, or how much you hate a specific thing that happened does nothing but create your reality opposite of what you want. That's where you'll find yourself in the same or similar situations. With the same people or even different people, you're the common denominator at the end of the day. Dealing with the same problems repeatedly causes you to endure the same emotions, producing the same thoughts, eventually resulting in the same behaviors that will keep you in the same place. That's why it's crucial to choose positivity, especially when it seems impossible.

You have to force positive thoughts by consciously thinking positive thoughts opposite to how you feel. For example, let's say you live in Minnesota and have just survived a long and brutal winter. It's April now; the sun is shining, birds are chirping, and you're getting a few rainy days. Now, the trees and flowers are blossoming and blooming. Then, in the middle of the month, you look out your window and see a blizzard. You instantly get upset and start verbalizing how mad you are that you have to go to work in a blizzard. You feel the anger building up and notice the words coming from your mouth. That moment is when you consciously think positive thoughts, even though you're feeling negative. The moment you decide to say, "Oh, how beautiful is the snow," "Good thing it'll be over 70 degrees for the rest of the week so that the snow will melt quickly", and "I'm going to have a great day today," you are guaranteed to come out of the negative mood and feelings you're experiencing. Intentional thinking works because it distracts your mind from your body. Instead of the body enduring the moment and controlling the mind, you're using your mind to control your body in the moment. Practice this as often as you can remember to.

Thoughts are things and can be a great neutralizer when you become aware of the thoughts that don't align with your divine purpose. Training your mind to think because of you and not for you will be difficult, uncomfortable, strange, and sometimes nearly impossible. You must commit to this practice to see a lasting and effective change. It's called a practice because it's repetitive. You have to keep working out to grow that muscle. You must commit to changing your mind to see more clearly to elevate yourself through and out of your circumstances.

It takes the sacrifice of our present selves to give in to a higher version of ourselves, which comes solely from a place of positivity, openness, and hope. Being positive will open up your mind, allowing positive thoughts and actions to reform your subconscious thinking. Your subconscious mind is your internal bank from which your thoughts, actions, and emotions derive. If you try to think positively and nothing's coming to mind, it's because you haven't deposited any positive thoughts into your subconscious bank. It's like going to the bank to withdraw a hundred dollars. Yet, you can't because you have no money or insufficient funds. Suppose you are continually actively depositing positive thoughts into your subconscious mind. In that case, they'll be there to use when you need to rely on your conscious thinking to get you through your situation. The same mind you are using to engage with this book is the one you need to use to think positive thoughts. If you believe you create your reality, you must understand and accept that your thoughts are creating it. Everything you've done and every action you've taken all started from a thought or an idea. Think about it. Just as you've used your mind to think and believe negatively, you can do the same to create a positive mindset.

For some people, it's too easy to dismiss the advice to "stay positive," "try to think positively," or "just be positive." It's almost as though they'd much rather stay in a negative space, complaining and wallowing in misery instead of accepting and embracing a more positive perspective. Choosing pain over peace will keep you in turmoil. Thinking more positively elevates your mood, makes finding and focusing on a solution to your problem more effortless, and motivates you to think more positively more often. It's that simple. If you think it's not that simple, ask yourself why. Is it because you don't want it to be? Would you rather life be more complex, dramatic, and chaotic? Or are you yearning for peace, genuine love, happiness, and success? What's stopping you from achieving it? Did you know your attitude about certain things sometimes makes them seem worse than they really are? Open yourself up to learning more about yourself. Become more aware of your thought patterns, emotions, and natural reactions. I emphasize mindfulness because that's what it takes to become aware of yourself well enough to know where you need to put the work in.

Do your actions match your intentions? Are you

making moves according to how you want your life to play out? What can you do today to elevate your attitude to match the desires of your heart? Suppose you remain focused on the negatives and simply refuse to be grateful amid your circumstances. In that case, even when someone gives you a more positive perspective or shows you a more significant way to view things, you are actively choosing to stay in misery instead of climbing your way out and intentionally choosing to not see the better side of your circumstance. Therefore, you are prolonging the outcome and continuing the same cycle. Humans are powerful because of what we can do with our minds. You have the power to change your life because you can change and use your mind. All it takes is the determination of a definite desire. That means, actively seeking ways to reach the desired outcome of your life. Let nothing and no one stop you from reaching your end goal. Notice, the more you learn about the abilities of your mind, the more results you produce, the more powerful you'll become, and the more positive circumstances you'll attract to your life. I am a prime example of this. Because I've been aware of and grateful for my mindset, my life is a direct reflection of me always thinking positively and believing in my mind's abilities. From meditation to writing, to just simply thinking big, I was able to transform my life and attract what some would call "good luck" or "miracles". I create my luck and attract miracles by opening myself up to the flow of abundance just by tapping into the power of my mind, and believing that I will receive exactly what I want in divine timing. As you tap into the power of your most powerful asset, watch your life significantly improve beyond your wildest dreams. Cheers to positivity! Sip, sip.

THE MIND

The mind is the most potent weapon humans possess. To not know that is to be unaware of the power within you. Do you know how many people reached success just by tapping into the powers of their minds? Too often, when we face adversities, our mind tends to wander in an adverse direction, causing us to react to the situation and become the feelings and emotions we experience instead of allowing us to remain calm enough to think effectively and focus on the solutions that will improve our circumstances. Do you know how easy it is and can be for you to resolve everyday issues if you consciously choose to think differently than usual? You have to actively think more positive thoughts and say more positive things, especially when you become aware of the negative thoughts and feelings that surface. Your mind is a weapon; your thoughts are ammo. The people in power who already possess this knowledge have used it to control the general population for centuries. Founding leaders led their followers based on their beliefs about themselves and their deep desires. They succeeded every time because they knew and understood the power of the mind. They knew the key to using their mind's power was to have a definite desire, a definite purpose for the things they pursue, trusting the process as they make the decisions that align with what they want and how they wish to live. Those who were unaware of the power within them were easily manipulated.

In the vast landscape of the human mind lie three distinct realms, each holding the key to our understanding, our growth, and our potential. These are the conscious, unconscious, and subconscious minds – the trio of our mental landscape, each playing a pivotal role in shaping our thoughts, emotions, and behaviors.

At the forefront of our consciousness lies the conscious mind, the beacon of awareness that illuminates our thoughts, desires, and actions. It is here that we deliberate, reason, and make decisions, wielding the power of intention and choice. Yet, beneath the surface, lie deeper currents of mental activity, unseen and often overlooked.

Descending into the depths of the unconscious mind, we encounter a vast reservoir of memories, emotions, and automatic responses. Like an invisible hand guiding our movements, the unconscious mind operates silently, shaping our behaviors and perceptions with its invisible influence. It is the warehouse of our past experiences, the keeper of our fears, and the architect of our habits.

But it is in the fertile soil of the subconscious mind that the seeds of transformation are sown. Here, amidst the tangle of neural pathways and synaptic connections, lies the power to reshape our reality. Like a sculptor molding clay, the subconscious mind shapes our beliefs, attitudes, and perceptions based on the experiences that have shaped our lives.

Yet, if we are unaware of the forces at play within our own minds, we risk becoming prisoners of our own unconscious programming. Unexamined beliefs, buried traumas, and hidden biases can shape our experiences in ways we may not fully comprehend, leading us down paths of self-sabotage and limitation.

But there is hope. For just as the mind can be a prison, it can also be a gateway to liberation. By cultivating mindfulness, self-awareness, and intentionality, we can unlock the hidden potentials of our subconscious minds and harness their power for personal growth and transformation.

Through practices such as positive affirmations, visualization, and hypnosis, we can access the hidden depths of our subconscious minds and reprogram the beliefs and behaviors that no longer serve us. By shining the light of awareness into the dark corners of our unconscious, we can release the grip of past traumas and outdated patterns, paving the way for a new dawn of possibility and potential.

So let us embark on this journey together, into the uncharted realms of our own minds. Let us explore the mysteries that lie within, and unlock the hidden potentials that await us. For in the depths of our own consciousness, lies the power to transform our lives, our relationships, and our world.

While the body has its natural processes and ways of doing things, our conscious mind interrupts them. For instance, the main problem humans have is the need to have complete control over everything. When that control is lost or not easily obtained, the mind follows in anger and frustration, causing most people to act out their thoughts and emotions. Self-control proves that you can use your mind to control your body and, therefore, control the outcome of your circumstances. Controlling yourself is more powerful and effective than trying to control the situation. For how you think and behave will always determine what happens next.

See the mind is not just a tool for processing information; it's a powerhouse of potential waiting to be unlocked. Yet, so many of us fail to grasp the immense power we wield within our own minds. Picture a vast reservoir of energy, waiting to be tapped into, waiting to be directed towards manifesting your deepest desires and wildest dreams. That's the potential that lies within you, waiting to be unleashed.

Think about it. How many success stories have you heard where individuals attribute their achievements to the power of their minds? From athletes visualizing their victories before they happen to entrepreneurs manifesting their dreams into reality, the power of the mind is undeniable. Yet, despite this knowledge, many of us continue to allow our minds to wander aimlessly, leading us down paths of doubt, fear, and negativity.

But it doesn't have to be this way. You have the power to take control of your mind and harness its full potential to create the life you desire. It starts with awareness – becoming conscious of the thoughts and emotions that are running through your mind at any given moment. When you catch yourself dwelling on negativity or self-doubt, pause and consciously choose to redirect your thoughts towards positivity and possibility.

One powerful mind hack is the practice of visualization. Close your eyes and imagine yourself achieving your goals with crystal clarity. See yourself succeeding, feel the emotions of accomplishment wash over you, and believe with every fiber of your being that it is possible. By visualizing your desired outcomes, you're programming your subconscious mind to work towards manifesting them into reality.

Another effective technique is affirmation. Repeat positive affirmations to yourself daily, affirming your worthiness, capabilities, and potential. By consistently feeding your mind with positive messages, you're reshaping your beliefs and programming your subconscious mind for success.

Furthermore, embrace the power of gratitude. Take time each day to reflect on the things you're grateful for, no matter how big or small. By focusing on the abundance in your life, you're shifting your mindset from one of lack to one of abundance, attracting even more blessings into your life.

Additionally, practice mindfulness to cultivate a greater sense of presence and awareness. Pay attention to the present moment, observing your thoughts and emotions without judgment. By staying grounded in the here and now, you're able to maintain clarity of mind and make more intentional choices. And perhaps most importantly, be kind to yourself. Understand that transformation takes time and patience, and that setbacks are a natural part of the process. Treat yourself with compassion and forgiveness, and celebrate your progress every step of the way.

In harnessing the power of your mind, you're not only transforming your own life, but you're also influencing the world around you. By radiating positivity, possibility, and abundance, you're inspiring others to do the same, creating a ripple effect of transformation and empowerment.

So, tap into the limitless potential of your mind, and watch as your life unfolds in ways you never thought possible. The power is within you – all you have to do is believe and take action. Sip-sip!

MONEY

In the big picture of life, money has a huge impact. It shapes our daily decisions, defines our social status, and often serves as a measure of our worth in the eyes of society. Yet, beneath the surface of this seemingly omnipotent force lies a complex web of myths, truths, and misconceptions that color our perceptions of wealth and poverty.

Myth: Rich people are inherently happier and more fulfilled than poor people.

Truth: While financial stability can certainly alleviate certain stresses and provide greater opportunities for comfort and leisure, true happiness and fulfillment does not depend upon wealth alone. Many studies have shown that beyond a certain threshold of income, additional wealth does not significantly increase levels of happiness.

Happiness is ultimately a state of mind, shaped by our relationships, our sense of purpose, and our ability to find meaning in our lives.

Myth: Poor people are lazy and lack ambition.

Truth: The reality is far more complex. While systemic barriers and economic inequalities can certainly contribute to cycles of poverty, many individuals living in poverty work tirelessly to make ends meet and provide for their families. Moreover, factors such as access to quality education, healthcare, and social support networks can play a significant role in determining one's economic opportunities and outcomes.

However, it's important to recognize that money, or the lack thereof, does present certain challenges and opportunities in our lives. For those struggling to make ends meet, financial insecurity can lead to stress, anxiety, and a sense of powerlessness. Basic necessities such as food, shelter, and healthcare may be out of reach, creating a cycle of deprivation that can be difficult to escape.

On the other hand, those who have accumulated wealth may find themselves grappling with a different set of challenges. The pursuit of wealth can become all-consuming, leading to a relentless pursuit of material possessions and status symbols. Relationships may suffer as priorities shift towards accumulating more wealth, and a sense of isolation and disconnection from others may arise.

So how do we navigate this complex landscape of money and its impact on our lives? How do we cultivate a healthier relationship with wealth and abundance, regardless of our current financial circumstances?

One powerful tool is self-reflection. Take a moment to examine your beliefs and attitudes towards money. How do you define success and prosperity? Are these definitions rooted in external markers such as wealth and possessions, or do they reflect deeper values and aspirations? By understanding our own motivations and desires, we can begin to align our actions with our true priorities and values.

Another important practice is gratitude. Take time each day to appreciate the abundance that already exists in your life, whether it's the love of family and friends, the beauty of nature, or the simple pleasures of everyday life. Cultivating an attitude of gratitude can shift our focus away from scarcity and lack towards abundance and possibility.

Furthermore, it's essential to cultivate a mindset of abundance rather than scarcity. Instead of dwelling on what we lack, focus on what we have and the opportunities that surround us. By adopting a mindset of abundance, we open ourselves up to new possibilities and attract more wealth and prosperity into our lives.

Finally, take practical steps to improve your financial literacy and management skills. Embarking on a journey to improve your financial literacy and management skills is a transformative step towards a brighter future. In the vast sea of financial concepts and strategies, it's easy to feel overwhelmed or unsure of where to begin. But fear not, for with dedication and perseverance, you can chart a course towards financial stability and prosperity.

First and foremost, arm yourself with knowledge. Explore the wealth of resources available at your fingertips, from books and articles to online courses and workshops. Dive into the fundamentals of budgeting, saving, investing, and debt management, equipping yourself with the tools you need to navigate the intricacies of personal finance.

Embarking on a journey to improve your financial literacy and management skills is not just about mastering the mechanics of budgeting and investing. It's also about cultivating a wealth mindset—a fundamental shift in how you perceive and approach money that lays the foundation for long-term wealth and prosperity.

At its core, a wealth mindset is about abundance—not just in terms of material wealth, but in all aspects of life. It's about recognizing and appreciating the abundance that already exists in your life, whether it's the love of family and friends, the beauty of nature, or the opportunities that surround you. By shifting your focus from scarcity to abundance, you open yourself up to new possibilities and attract more wealth and prosperity into your life.

A wealth mindset is also about taking ownership of your financial destiny. Instead of playing the role of victim, blaming external circumstances or others for your financial woes, you recognize that you have the power to shape your own financial future. You take responsibility for your financial decisions and actions, knowing that each choice you make has the potential to move you closer to—or further from—your financial goals.

Moreover, a wealth mindset is about embracing risk and seeing failure as an opportunity for growth. Instead of being paralyzed by fear of failure or loss, you understand that taking calculated risks is an essential part of building wealth. You recognize that failure is not the end of the road, but rather a stepping stone on the path to success. You learn from your mistakes, adapt, and persevere, knowing that setbacks are temporary and that every failure brings you one step closer to your goals.

A wealth mindset is about generosity and giving back. It's about recognizing that true wealth is not just about accumulating material possessions, but about making a positive impact in the lives of others. Whether it's through charitable giving, volunteering, or simply offering support and encouragement to those in need, you understand that true wealth is measured not by what you have, but by what you give.

As you cultivate a wealth mindset, you'll find that your relationship with money—and with life itself—begins to transform. You'll approach financial decisions with confidence and clarity, knowing that you have the tools and resources to achieve your goals. You'll attract opportunities for growth and abundance into your life, and you'll find fulfillment not just in what you have, but in who you are and what you contribute to the world.

So as you embark on your journey to improve your financial literacy and management skills, remember to also cultivate a wealth mindset. Embrace abundance, take ownership of your financial destiny, embrace risk and failure as opportunities for growth, and give back generously. By doing so, you'll not only build long-term wealth and prosperity for yourself, but you'll also create a legacy of abundance and generosity that will enrich the lives of others for generations to come.

Once you've laid the groundwork, it's time to put your wealth-mindset into action. Start, by creating a budget that reflects your income, expenses, and financial goals. Track your spending habits, identify areas where you can cut back or save more, and allocate your resources wisely to ensure you are living within your means.

Saving regularly is a cornerstone of financial stability. Set up automatic transfers from your checking account to a dedicated savings account, building up an emergency fund to cover unexpected expenses and saving for future goals like homeownership, education, or retirement. Another way to remember to save, which is a method I love the most, is by adding yourself to your list of bills and paying yourself first. This means taking 10–20 percent from every check and putting it into a savings account or keeping it as emergency cash on hand. Remember, every dollar saved is a step closer to financial freedom.

As you gain confidence in your ability to manage your finances, consider tackling any outstanding debt you may have. Prioritize high-interest debt and explore strategies like the debt snowball or avalanche method to pay it off efficiently. With each payment, you'll inch closer to a debt-free future and liberate yourself from the burden of interest charges.

Investing for the future is another essential aspect of financial literacy. Educate yourself about different investment options and risk levels, and consider diversifying your portfolio to minimize risk and maximize returns. Whether you're investing in stocks, bonds, mutual funds, or real estate, remember to align your investments with your long-term financial goals and risk tolerance. Staying informed is key to staying ahead in the ever-evolving landscape of personal finance. Keep abreast of financial news and developments that may impact your financial situation, and seek out trusted sources of information and advice. Consider consulting with a certified financial planner or advisor for personalized guidance tailored to your unique circumstances and goals.

In the end, remember that improving your financial literacy and management skills is a journey, not a destination. Celebrate your progress, learn from your mistakes, and stay committed to your financial goals. With determination and perseverance, you can achieve financial stability and unlock a world of opportunities for yourself and your loved ones.

In conclusion, money is a powerful force that shapes our lives in profound ways. By understanding the myths and truths surrounding wealth and poverty, cultivating a wealth mindset and a healthier relationship with money, and taking practical steps to improve our financial well-being, we can transform our lives and create a future of abundance and prosperity.

Chapter Nine

CLOSING REMARKS

In the closing pages of this journey, may you find yourself not at an end, but at a beginning —an inception of your truest self, unfurling like a blossom in the warmth of self-love and self-awareness.

Amidst the tumultuous landscape of life, where shadows of doubt and despair may loom, remember this: you are the architect of your destiny, the weaver of your own tapestry. In the depths of darkness, you possess the light to illuminate your path forward. Embrace the intricacies of your being—the flaws and the brilliance, the scars and the triumphs. For it is in accepting the entirety of who you are that you unlock the door to profound self-discovery.

In the crucible of depression, know that you are not alone. Reach out, for there is solace in connection, and strength in vulnerability. Allow yourself to be supported, to be seen, to be loved. Harness the boundless power of your mind, for within its vast expanse lies the potential to shape your reality. Cultivate positivity, nurture resilience, and watch as the universe conspires to manifest your deepest desires.

In the currency of relationships, invest wholeheartedly. Treasure the bonds that uplift and inspire, for they are the pillars upon which the structure of your life stands tall. And as for money—recognize its significance, but do not let it define your worth. True wealth resides not in material possessions, but in the richness of experience, the abundance of love, and the generosity of spirit.

So, dear reader, as you turn the final page, know that this is not the end, but a new beginning—a genesis of possibility, a journey towards wholeness. May you walk forth with courage in your heart, with purpose in your stride, and with the unwavering belief that within you lies the power to create a life of extraordinary beauty and fulfillment. Sip-sip!

Chapter Ten

MESSAGE TO MY READERS

As I pen these final words, my heart swells with gratitude for you, dear reader. It's with profound appreciation that I reflect on the journey we've embarked upon together—a journey of self-discovery, resilience, and growth.

Through the pages of this book, I've shared not only insights and practices but also pieces of my own soul. It's through the crucible of my own life's trials and triumphs that these mind hacks and practices have been forged. I am deeply grateful for the opportunity to impart them to you, knowing firsthand the transformative power they hold.

As I look back on my own path, I am filled with awe at the resilience of the human spirit. Despite the storms that have raged, I have persevered, guided by the light of self-awareness and the unwavering belief in my own abilities.

And now, as I stand at the culmination of this endeavor, I am humbled by the realization that every challenge, every setback, has been a stepping stone leading me to this moment. I am grateful for the opportunity to share the fruits of my journey with you, knowing that in doing so, I have fulfilled a purpose greater than myself.

So, to you, my dear reader, I extend my deepest thanks. Thank you for embarking on this odyssey with me, for allowing me to be a part of your journey. May the wisdom contained within these pages serve as a guiding light, illuminating your path to a life of profound fulfillment and joy.

Peace, Love and Prosperity to you all! Sip-sip!

www.ingramcontent.com/pod-product-compliance
Lightning Source LLC
Chambersburg PA
CBHW061356140726
47997CB00003B/1230